Kiev

The Essential Kiev Guide
2018 Edition

Alina Potter

ISBN 9781977004000

A GO2UA.com publication

CONTENTS

CONTENTS

INTRODUCTION

The Essential Kiev Guide (2018 Edition) has been revised and updated to introduce Kiev's key sights, experiences and travel essentials to make your stay in the Ukrainian capital and enjoying and exciting one.

Our experience as one of Kiev's leading tour operators for western visitors has helped us craft a book which we hope we offer practical advice and useful tips when navigating our city and its many attractions.

The 2018 edition includes Things to Do, maps to help you navigate the city and metro and an expanded Essentials section.

For visitors wish to have a tour guide while visiting Kiev we invite you to visit www.go2ua.com for more information.

We wish you a warm and enjoyable stay in our friendly city.

Naslazhdat'sya. Enjoy!
Alina Potter

HISTORY

Kiev. The heart of Ukraine.

Kiev capital of Ukraine is for most the gateway to Ukraine. The Ukrainian capital, on the banks of the Dnepr river, has a population of 3.2 million, rising to 4 million in wider metropolitan area, making it one of Europe's ten largest cities.

Kiev is a rich city of contrast and beauty from art nouveau architecture to magnificent orthodox churches to imposing monuments to its Soviet past.

Kiev has been at the crossroads of history for centuries and this fusion of Greek, Slavic, Scandinavian, western and Russian influence is in evidence everywhere.

Many of the Kiev's oldest buildings are over fifteen centuries old with over 2000 sites of historical and cultural importance and 39 of international importance.

Kiev has historically been one of the most important economic, political, scientific, religious and cultural centers in eastern Europe. The Ukrainian capital was the seat of power of the Kiev-Rus (882-1240AD), a mighty east Slavic federation, a sprawling empire spanned from the Black Sea in the south to the Baltic Sea in the arctic north.

Kiev is the capital not only of Ukraine, but of Slavic civilization.

Tens of thousands of tourists flock to Kiev every year to enjoy the capital's rich history and culture. Kiev boasts over 100 museums, 140 libraries, 33 theaters and over 50 houses of culture, including:

Kiev's iconic St. Sophia Cathedral, built in 1021, is an architectural masterpiece that attracts the attention of tourists from all over the world. It was here, in Ukraine's capital, were the first library was founded by Prince Yaroslav the Wise. Entry: USD 3.00.

St. Andrew's Church, built in a more familiar western European architecture with unique Ukrainian features in 1749 by architect Bartolomeo Rastrelli.

Kiev-Pechersk Lavra (Kiev Cave monastery) is the spiritual masterpiece of Kievan Rus period. Monks would write books, paint, sing and prescribe medicine in the sanctity and safety of the church. Entry: USD 2.00.

The Golden Gate, Mariinskiy Palace, popular National Opera and Ballet Theatre are among other must-see destination for any visitor to Kiev.

Kiev or Kyiv?

The English interpretation of the Ukraine's capital city has been the subject of debate in recent years.

Kyiv and Kiev are in frequent use.

The variation in spelling arises from the translation from Ukrainian and Russian. Historically the Russian interpretation, Kiev, dominated however since Ukrainian independence in 1991 the newly sovereign nation recognized Ukrainian as an official language and the chose to adopt the native spelling to its capital, Kyiv.

Many countries, in solidarity with the Ukrainian authorities, recognized new interpretation and formally adopted Kyiv.

In 2006 the United States government formally recognized Kyiv, in support of the independent Ukraine state.

United States Representative, Tom Casey, said that the Office of Geographic Names decreed that Kyiv will be recognized as the official name for the Ukrainian capital all federal agencies. Congress ratified the changes in a move which saw many international organizations, including NATO and the United Nations also recognise the new designation.

Despite the international recognition some countries have been slow to adopt Kyiv.

Kiev is still in regular usage in the United Kingdom, however since the revolution in 2014 and Russian aggression in Crimea the British authorities have adopted the Ukrainian spelling, Kyiv.

KIEV SIGHTSEEING

Kreschatik Street

Kreschatik (Khreschatyk) is the 1.5km long main street of Kiev and a must-see for visitors. The beautiful street plays host to many celebrations and events and is often referred to as the Kievan Champs Elysees. The boulevard is closed to vehicles on the weekends giving Kievans the freedom of the street.

If you're an eager shopper be sure to visit the vast Globus Commercial Center which boasts almost 200 shops on three levels, under Independence Square at the northern end of Kreschatik.

Kreschatik is home to exclusive brands like Gucci, Dolce & Gabbana, Roberto Cavalli, and popular high street names including Zara, Desigual, Diesel, Adidas and Mango.

While if you're interested in a more authentic taste of Kiev try the Besarabsky Market at the southern end of Kreschatik and sample the finest fresh Kievan produce, Kiev's oldest market.

During WWII the Soviets laid mines here to trap the advancing German army. The scale of the minefield led many buildings to exploding or burning down which is why today many buildings on Kreschatik have Stalinist architecture from being rebuilt in post-war period.

Independence Square (Majdan Nezalezhnosti)

This 200 year old square is the main meeting place in the city and country and events here have helped shape the country's past and present. The Square has been the site of many of Ukraine's most important cultural and political events in recent years.

On the left side of the square is a Monument of Independence, symbolizing the freedom of the country (see photograph above).

Further to the left a monument of city's founders stands, three brothers, Kie, Shchek, Khoriv and their sister Lebid. Legend has it Kiev was named after the oldest brother Kiy.

Independence Square is one of the most popular areas for tourists with many hotels, shops and amenities all close by.

St. Sophia's Cathedral

St. Sophia's Cathedral, Kiev's oldest church, was named a UNESCO world heritage site in 1990, recognizing its beauty and global cultural significance.

Stunning original mosaics and frescoes date from 1017 when the cathedral was built to honor Prince Yaroslav's victory over invading tribes.

St. Sophia's striking golden dome and 76m (250ft) bell tower were baroque flourishes added in the 18th century.

The Cathedral and grounds are another must-see attraction in Kiev.

Grounds open 9am-7pm daily. Cathedral 10am-6pm Thursday-Tuesday, 10am-5pm Wednesday.

Cave Monastery of Kiev

The 1000 year old Cave Monastery dazzles visitors with its beauty and history, with striking views to the Dnieper

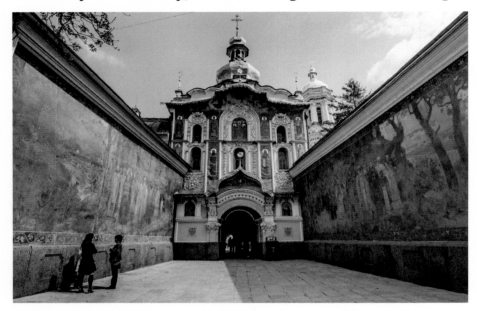

river and cave tunnels. The Monastery was founded in 1051 by monk Antony and his disciple Theodosius. The building was mentioned in the 12th century in the writing of Nestor the Chronicler, a monk and author of "The Tale of Bygone Years". The magnificent Monastery grounds span over 40 hectares (100 acres).

The sacred site was a centre of medicine and the site of the first Kiev Rus hospital, The first books were written on this site, and the first art school as also formed here.

The Bell Tower which soars to 96m (315 ft) was once the tallest bell tour in Ukraine and in ancient times legend has it could be heard from 250km (150mi).

The caves, constructed in the 11th century, over almost 100 years, are over 800m long and were once home to monks who lived and prayed there.

The Cave Monastery is a must see destination for any visitor to Kiev.

St Michael's Cathedral

The Cathedral was found in 1108 and destroyed in 1937 while the country was under soviet control before being lovingly restored in 1998. Before the destruction of the Cathedral scientists removed from the walls treasured mosaics and frescoes made by famous masters of Kievan Rus many centuries earlier.

The history of the church may be explored in the monastery bell tower on the grounds, where the tale of destruction under Soviet rule is explained in English.

Golden Gate Kiev

The Gate is the ancient entrance to the city built in 1164 following the construction of defensive walls of the new city. The imposing structure impresses with its grandeur and inaccessibility: presided over by a powerful military tower and housing the Church of the Annunciation.

The architectural style of the gate, built by Prince Vladimir, was totally different from similar structures erected by architects in Europe. European structures provided defensive

function mainly, represented as simple towers while Golden Gate in Kiev, rather can be compared with the triumphant Golden Gate in Constantinople. Kiev Golden Gate served as an entrance tower and a triumphal arch at the same time, which led to the main "aristocratic street" of the city. High arched doorway, being bound in gilded copper gate and head gate of the temple created a proper festive atmosphere.

Tickets: USD 1.40 for adults.

Kiev Opera

Kiev Opera and Ballet Theater (Kiev Opera) is an architectural monument to the 19th century. In 1898, after a fire in 1896, the construction of a new building began under Russian architect Viktor Schröter.

Performances held from September through to June. Tickets: USD 2.00 to USD 75.00 depending on the performance time and seat choice.

Pirogovo Museum

This open air museum, located 12km (7.5 miles) south of Kiev is one of the capital's top attractions, situated on the outskirts of city over 150 hectares (370 acres) of forest and parkland.

The Museum grounds house more than 300 buildings, each reflecting the traditional historical regions of Ukraine dating from the 17th-19th century. The authentic houses and churches where transported from every region of Ukraine and loving rebuild here at Pirogovo to create a perfect replica of Ukrainian life. Interiors, gardens, yards from across the country and throughout the centuries. A visit to Pirogovo will transport you through time to yesteryear.

Pirogovo includes one zone which recreates Soviet villages of 1970's to provide a contrast between life under Soviet rule and Ukraine today. History buffs will delight in the rich social, culture and economic tapestry on display at this vast unique museum.

The official name of the Museum is "National Museum of Folk Architecture and Life" locally has given way to the simpler and more imaginative name, Pirogovo Museum, reflecting the name of the village, which existed in this region from the seventeenth century.

In the summer traditional arts, crafts and historical activities such as wood carving and pottery are undertaken to recreate an authentic taste of yesteryear. In just a few hours visitors can same a taste of history and sample the cuisine, crafts and culture from across the country.

Pirogovo also hosts many festivals thorough the year and musicians play every weekend.

Entry: USD 1.50, Golf-car 1 hour tour: USD 14.00 for 2 persons.

Kiev Rus Park

Kyiv Rus Park is open-air entertaining museum celebrating Kiev Rus culture and history. It is a cultural center of east-Slavic countries and is a unique tourist attraction for those interested in the region's rich history and evolution of the Slavic culture.

The creators of Rus Park have reproduced an architectural image of ancient Kyiv from V-XIII centuries in 1:1 scale and recreated the atmosphere of Kievan Rus, applying the real facts and scientific data.

Ticket Price: Adults USD 5.00, children USD 1.50.

War Museum

The World War II museum (also known as Great Patriotic War museum) houses more than 300,000 unique exhibits in both indoor and outdoor collections of tanks, weapons and firearms, awards, battle flags, documentary photographs, letters and diaries of wartime objects of everyday life, powerfully chronicling wartime.

During summer period you may also enjoy a trip to the top of the motherland statue top (103 meters high) to have a

spectacular bird's eye view of the sprawling city.

The exhibition presents both Soviet and Nazi war artefacts.

Tickets: Main exposition entry: USD 0.70, Motherland statue lift: USD 8.00.

House with Khimeras

Decorated with bizarre sculptures of animals and mammals this famous Kiev attraction resembles a masterpiece, transplanted from the peaked roof of the Notre-Dame in Paris and transported to Kiev. The House with Khimeras is both the current residence of the Ukrainian President and an architectural museum of unusual Kievan creation. The roof of the building is decorated with rows of good-natured toads. From the walls of the house heads of rhinos and antelopes spring forward, while water pipes are made in

the form of snakes and elephant trunks. One more surprise, this grand cliff top house appears to have only 3 floors from the front but the back reveals six!

Many legends have accompanied the House with Khimeras during construction but in reality it was just smart advertising campaign launched by architecture Gorodetsky to promote a new material. Concrete.

As an official residence of the Ukrainian President access to the House with Khimeras is now limited. Tickets are available via online queue on Saturday every week.

Ticket Price: USD 2.50.

Chernobyl Museum

Dedicated to the Chernobyl catastrophe on 26 April 1986, the museum chronicles the causes and consequences of the accident. The Museum contains photographs, relics from the exclusion zone, declassified documents, maps and a three-phase diorama of Chernobyl nuclear power plant before, during and after the accident. The museum serves as a shrine to the human cost of the nuclear accident and the aftermath of the explosion of Chernobyl power plant reactor No 4, over thirty years ago.

The haunting exhibits are described in Russian and Ukrainian however English-speaking visitors will find a limited number of English-language audio guides are available.

Tours to the site of the disaster are also available. See Chernobyl Tour below.

Open: 10am-6pm, Monday-Saturday. Entry: USD 0.70.

Tours to Chernobyl and Prypiat

Visitors to Kiev frequently make the short trip north to the site of the infamous 1986 nuclear explosion in Chernobyl. Tours are permitted only by authorised agencies and special monitoring equipment is used monitor radiation for your safety. Those wishing to visit Chernobyl will be required to register with passport details and make a booking 4-5 days in advance as clearance must be sought from the state security service.

St Andrew Descent (Andriyivsky Uzviz)

St Andrew's Descent is a unique place. A market street of arts, crafts and souvenirs where many artists display their work. Historically, Andrew's Descent connected the government district of city with Podil, the commercial merchant center. Now it is Kievits' favorite destination for outdoor fairs, festivals and concerts. Travellers come here to visit art-galleries, shops and studios. Here you will see a great selection of various souvenirs, antiques and paintings.

Mariinskiy Palace and Park

Mariinskiy Park, close to the very centre of Kiev, is a green picturesque place. You can walk along its paths, admire beautiful fountains, listen to talented street musicians or take a seat on one of the benches under big old trees, welcome respite during hot summer afternoons.

Mariinskiy Park differs from all others with its incomparable scenery on Dnieper River.

You may want to stay here for hours, in the very centre of the city, surrounded by trees, looking at famous river and its bridges, with a royal palace behind.

National Philharmonic

National Philharmonic of Ukraine has been hosting concerts since 1863, when the first Kiev branch of the Imperial Russian Musical Society was founded.

Performances are supported by the National Symphony Orchestra and other classical music bands presenting music from famous composers such as Rachmaninoff, Bach, Mozart, Shubert, Shuman, Wagner and many others.

THINGS TO DO

Cultural Performances

Kiev has a rich and popular artistic tradition with musical and cultural performances held year round at the many theatres in the city.

Tickets and information on events can be found on the english edition of these websites: https://concert.ua/en; http://parter.ua/; https://karabas.com/en/.

Among the highlights on the Kiev cultural calendar are:

A series of summer concerts are held on UBK (Uzhniy Bereg Kieva) or the south bank on the Dniper river in Kiev on Trukhanov Island.

New Year concerts are very popular with the locals and always well attended. Look out for favourites Tysiacha Ogney (Thousand Lights) and Vartovi Mrij (Dreams Guards).

Opera and Ballet performances are held at the National Opera & Ballet Theatre in the city center. The National Opera company, which marked it's 150th anniversary in

2017, performs perennial favourites Swan Lake, Nutcracker, Carmen and Romeo & Juliet are regularly alongside traditional Ukrainian plays. For the full program and to purchase tickets visit the Opera online at https://www.opera.com.ua/en/.

The National Philharmonic Orchestra hosts classical concerts at venues in downtown Kiev throughout the year. The Orchestra returns to the capital in 2018 fresh from a tour of the United States. Performance tickets typically range from USD 2.50 to USD 10.70 and can be purchased from the Orchestra's website http://www.filarmonia.com.ua/en.

Key Addresses:
National Opera House, *50 Volodymyrska St, Kiev*
National Palace of Arts, *103 Velyka Vasylkivska St, Kiev*
International Center of Culture and Arts,
1 Heroyiv Nebesnoyi Sotni Alley, Kiev
National Philharmonic of Ukraine
2 Volodymyrs'kyi Descent

Beach Clubs

Kievans flock beach clubs in the warm summer months and enjoy the relaxed atmosphere and holiday vibe. The beach clubs feature music, swimming pool and chaise longues for relaxing. The cost of admission varies between USD 10-20 depending on the club and day of the week. Weekend admission prices are higher.

Some of the local favourites include Olmeca Plage (5m Brovarskoy Boulevard), Sky Family Park (SkyMall Shopping Mall, 2 Generala Vatutina Boulevard) and the Sandali Resort on Trukhanov Island.

Bike Rentals

Sporty types may enjoy renting a bike on Trukhanov Island, the large island to the east of the city centre in the Dniper river. Trukhanov is a popular escape for locals with island in an easy 15 min walk from Maidan Square across a footbridge. Bikes may be rented for a day or by the hour.

For more information contact:
Amigo Bikes
Telephone: +380 66 512 9555
Website: http://amigostour.kiev.ua/
Email: amigostour@bigmir.net

Climb the Motherland Statue

In the summer months for the more adventurous, a visit to the War Museum wouldn't be complete without climbing the soviet-era Motherland Statue which dominates the skyline in the south of the city and soars to 62m (203 ft) over the city. The statue hold a sword in the right hand which rises to 16m (52ft) high and weighs a hefty 9 tons! The left hand carries a shield of the Soviet Union.

The Motherland Statue has two viewing levels which can be scaled in the summer months only for USD 1.80 for the lower reaches or USD 7.10 for willing climbers to reach the higher viewing platform.

Address: Zapecherna St, Kiev

Shooting

Shooting is a popular pursuit in Ukraine and gun lovers will enjoy the city's rifle ranges and the range of weaponry to try.

Anyone wishing to visit a shooting range should take a valid passport as identification. Licenses are not required when shooting on a registered range in the presence of a licensed operator.

Ukraine Expocenter (VDNKh)

The Expo center (http://www.expocenter.com.ua/) in city's south hosts a variety of events and exhibitions and is home to a popular shooting range where visitors can use three types of weapons, AK47, Mosina rifle and TT gun. Address: VDNKh, Hlushkova Boulevard, 1, Kiev.

Sapsan

Sapsan (http://sapsan.ua/), 20 minutes drive from Kiev, is a professional shooting range with a wide variety of pistols and semi-automatic firearms available for hire. Address: 29 Chklalova Street, Brovary.

TOURS

Go2UA (www.go2ua.com, Tel: +38(097)9466549, Email: welcome@go2ua.com.) is a specialist travel services provider in Ukraine. We welcome visitors every week from Europe and North America and provide personal tours, transport and translation services for the leisure and business traveler.

If you're considering a visit to Kiev we invite you to join us on one of our many tours of beautiful Kiev. Here's a small selection of our specialist interest tours.

Mezhigirja Palace

A 20km trip from Kiev, the home of the disgraced former Ukrainian President is an impressive monument to his time in power. The 150 hectare (370 acre) grounds and four floor Palace, was home until he fled after the revolution in 2013. Today the home and grounds, which once were a country reserve, before being commandeered by the former President, has again been returned to the Ukrainian people and is a national park.

Lovingly maintained by volunteers, this monument of wealth demonstrates to Ukrainians how government money was misappropriated and how a gap between rich and poor was created. The palace is colloquially called the "Museum of Corruption" by Ukrainians.

Entry: 8 USD with house entry.

Boat trip on Dnepr River

Experience Kiev's beauty from the hills and Cathedrals golden domes, rich history and ancient cultural and trade center of the capital of Ukraine on a boat trip on the Dnepr River which winds its way through the capital.

Accompanied by a private guides you will learn about the city's rich history and recent renaissance.

Entry: USD 4-5, 1 hour boat trip departing every hour from Kontractova Square.

Gastronomical Delights Tour

Sample four national dishes at four authentic Ukrainian restaurants with our gastronomic guide in the heat of Kiev. You will enjoy each dish with a uniquely Ukrainian aperitif before eating visiting the next restaurant on your culinary tour.

Arts & Folk Pirogovo Museum

Relax in over 150 hectares (370 acres) and step back in time to sample 300 years of history at the incredible outdoor museum which features traditional houses from across Ukraine.

We'll pass through the old windmills, school, churches buildings from 19th century, and experience history. Ukrainian tableware, furniture, interior, national outfit, food and drinks is all represented in one place and faithfully recreated at Pirogovo. Entry: USD 1.10. Tours: Tel: +38(097)9466549, Email: welcome@go2ua.com.

Jewish Tour

Discover the history of the Jewish community is Kiev with your personal guide including the story of Babij Yar.

In the late summer of 1941 as the Nazis rolled eastwards across Ukraine during the height of WW2 the occupying force rounded up Kiev's 34,000 Jews and marched them to Babyn Yar ravine where all were horrifically massacred over 48 hours by the Nazi oppressors. The helpless victims were shot and buried in the ravine in one of the most horrific war crimes of World War II. Thousands more Kievans were to die at Babyn Yar in the two years that followed as the site became Syrets Concentration Camp.

The true scale of the atrocities at Babyn has only become known since the war and following Ukrainian independence in 1991 the site is now properly commemorated with a Jewish memorial, a menorah and ten years later with a second monument to commemorate the children who died at Babyn Yar was erected.

Today, more than 70 years after these horrors, Kyiv again has a thriving 60,000 strong Jewish community.

TOURIST ESSENTIALS

Airlines

As the gateway to Ukraine, Kiev is well served by international airlines. The city's two international airports, Borispol Airport, in the city's east and Zhuliany Airport in the south, have regular scheduled flights to continental Europe and beyond.

Borispol also serves as the main hub for Ukraine International Airlines (UIA) which has an extensive international route network from the capital's main airport.

Zhuliany, the city airport, is popular with low-cost airlines while Kiev's Borispol International Airport is a popular destination for major carriers.

International airlines flying from North America and Asia will typically require transit in western Europe prior to the onward journey to Kiev.

Many of world's best known airlines have regular scheduled flights to Kiev Borispol including Air France,

Austrian Airlines, British Airways, Czech Airlines, KLM, LOT, Lufthansa, Turkish Airlines and Ukrainian International Airlines.

Low-cost carriers service Zhuliany include Alitalia, flydubai, LOT, Vueling and WizzAir.

For flight information and fares to Kiev we recommend momondo.com.

Airports

Kiev is served by two international airports. Boryspil (or Borispol – Russian spelling), Ukraine's largest and busiest airport in the city's east and Zhuliany airport to the south in the city. While Borispol is a central international airport, Zhuliany is smaller and used mainly by the budget airlines.

Borispol International Airport (KBP) is located 35 km from central Kiev with excellent transport links via the MO3 motorway. The motorway, which is a major intercity highway, can be congested so allow 30-80 minutes for a trip to the city centre depending on the traffic.

The airport was built for the 2012 European Football Championships co-hosted by Ukraine so passengers today enjoy facilities and amenities expected of any modern airport.

Public buses shuttles are easy to find just in front of the arrival hall exit.

SkyBus offers a direct service from the airport to the central railing station in the city. The bus operates every 15 minutes in peak times and every 45 minutes off peak. Tickets are available online, but we recommend to purchase in the local hryvnia currency on the bus. For more information and timetables visit http://skybus.kiev.ua/en/.

Hire cars and taxis are available in the arrival hall, however tourists can be overcharged by overzealous taxi touts so pre-booked airport transfers are recommend.

Kiev's second airport, Zhuliany (IEV), is located 10km south of the city centre. Since 2000 the airport has enjoyed steady growth and many low cost carriers, including Wizz Air and Vueling, now serve the airport. Transfers to city hotels will take 25-45 minutes depending on local traffic conditions.

Zhuliany is not served by the metro so those looking to travel into the city will need to book a taxi or take TrolleyBus 9 to the LVA Tolstogo Square metro station where you can ride the metro into the city. Trolleybus tickets are available for purchase on the bus.

When ordering a taxi from Zhuliany Airport be sure to identify the terminal (see Taxi section) as drivers can often arrive at the wrong terminal.

Official city tourist information centres are conveniently located in the arrival hall at both airports and will be able to assist you with local travel and transport advice, free maps and other helpful basic useful information to make your stay more pleasant.

For airport transfers contact Go2UA.

Tel: +38(097)9466549, Web: www.go2ua.com, Email: welcome@go2ua.com.

Business Hours

Hours of business vary however it in general Kievans recognise the following business hours.

Banks & offices: 9am-5pm or 10am-6pm
Shops: 9am-6pm, larger central city shops to 8-9pm
Restaurants: noon-11pm
Tourist Sights: 9am-5pm or 6pm, closed one day a week

It is not common for shops to close on Sunday.

Climate

Kiev experiences moderately cold winters (average min: -6°C, 21°F) and enjoys warm summers (average max: 25°C, 78°F). Usually it feels like a very hot summer and high humidity and extremely cold winter with lots of wind, snow and -15°C/5°F.

The ideal seasons to visit the Ukrainian capital are mid-April through June when the blossoms are in bloom and before the heat of summer or in September and early October as the leaves start to fall and the summer turns to autumn.

In July, the hottest month, visitors should be sure not to miss the popular Kiev beach clubs which are either by the river side or in the forests, with food, chez long and beach volleyball courts.

During July and August, in the height of summer, Kiev

can experience thunderstorms and brief downpours accompanying the warmer weather.

By October and November rainfall increases before the cooler temperatures bring the winter snow. Snow is frequent from mid-November through March before giving way to warmer spring temperatures.

See the What to Wear section for more information.

Co-Working Spaces

Co-working spaces are popular for entrepreneurs and startups in Kiev and many offer affordable day rates for casual visitors. If you're in Kiev on business and looking for handy business base during your stay or conduct meetings then one of Kiev's many co-working spaces could be a good option.

Chasopys Hub

Our favourite co-working space with great facilities, English speaking staff and excellent coffee.
Address: 4 floor, 3 Lva Tolstogo St
Email: coworking@chasopys.kiev.ua
Web: http://coworking.chasopys.ua/en/
Telephone: +380 95 20 686 21

Fedoriv

Fedoriv is located adjacent to the Arena City and entertainment complex at the end of Kreschatik Street, Kiev's major street.
Address: 5th floor, Velyka Vasylkivska St, 5
Email: hub@fedoriv.com
Web: http://fedoriv.com/hub/
Telephone: +380 44 281 44 55

i-HUB Coworking
Centrally located co-working space on the main Kiev street.
Web: http://ihub.world/en/
Address: 10, Kreschatik St
Telephone: +380 50 334 7240

Hub 4.0
A coworking space located in the trendy riverside Podil district.
Telephone: +38050 468 4040
Address: 1/3 Yaroslavskiy Provulok

Electricity

Ukraine uses the continental European style two pin electricity sockets. The standard voltage is 220V and the standard frequency is 50 Hz.

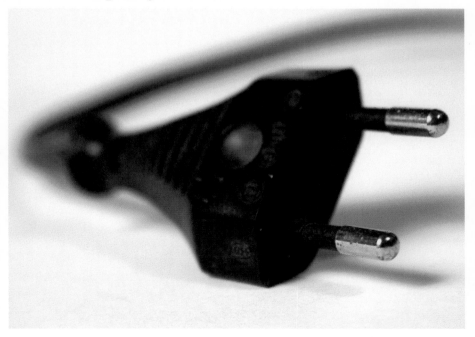

Hotels don't offer electrical adaptors so visitors will need to bring them or buy on arrival. We would recommend ordering adapters before you depart.

EU/Ukrainian power adapters can be purchased inexpensively on Amazon, for US plugs (USD10.99, buy http://amzn.to/2jWkVXd) and UK plugs (GBP5.24 on Amazon, buy http://amzn.to/2jWimEu).

For those needing to purchase adapters in Kiev try Citrus (citrus.ua) and Foxtrot (foxtrot.com.ua) electrical stores in Kiev which may stock adapters however for peace of mind we recommend visitors bring them to Ukraine.

Embassies

In emergencies foreign nationals should contact their Embassy in Kiev.

Embassy (UK)	00380 44 490 3660
Embassy (USA)	00380 44 521 5000
Embassy (France)	00380 44 590 3600
Embassy (Germany)	00380 44 247 6800
Embassy (Netherlands)	00380 44 490 8200
Embassy (Italy)	00380 44 230 3100
Embassy (Poland)	00380 44 230 0700
Embassy (Canada)	00380 44 590 3100
Embassy (Australia)	00380 44 290 6400

Food & Drink

No visit to Kiev is complete without sampling some traditional Ukrainian cuisine. Here are some the Kievan favorite dishes you can expect to find at many restaurants across the city.

Borsch

Ukraine's most famous dish. A delicious sour red soup full of meat and vegetables. The red color comes from beetroot, on of the core ingredients of Ukrainian borsch. The dish is usually made with meat and vegetables such as cabbage, carrots, onions, potatoes and tomatoes. Borsch may be served hot or cold and is often served with sour cream. Every family in Ukraine has its own unique recipe and the soup has many regional variants. Meat stock, vegetable choices and style of vegetable cuts vary throughout the country. In Kiev mutton, lamb and beef are most commonly used while in other regions poultry is more common.

Vareniki

Vareniki, or crescent shaped dumplings, are another popular and versatile Ukrainian dish served as an everyday meal and as part of traditional celebrations.

Vareniki are typically filled with either savory fillings: a variety of fillings such as mashed potato, fried onions, ground meat and cabbage or sweet fillings, cherry, strawberry, raspberry, fresh white cheese. Over 100 types of Vareniki dumplings with a many fillings are available. They are often served with sour cream and butter.

Kovbasa
Kovbasa describes various kinds of smoked or boiled pork, beef or chicken sausage which you will find in plentiful supply across Kiev.

Holubtsi
Holubtsi is a cabbage roll, with fresh or sour cabbage leaves wrapped a rice filling with meat -- minced beef or bacon -- and lightly baked in old and caramelized onions. It is popular to cook Holubtsi in tomato juice, sauce or paste. The dish is garnished with spices and seasoning and may also be serviced with bacon dripping or roasted and adorned with bacon strips.

Interested in sampling more delicious Ukrainian dishes before your visit? We recommend the cookbook Mamushka: Recipes from Ukraine & beyond available from Amazon (USD6.99 http://amzn.to/2jKHa1I, GBP9.99 http://amzn.to/2iMA2lY) to whet your appetite for Ukrainian food.
For more information on the dining out in Kiev please see the Restaurants section.

Foreign Media
Kiev's finest hotels offer satellite television channels, typically including BBC News, CNN, Rai, Deutsche Welle.
The free Kyiv Post is an English language published every

Friday and available at cafes and restaurants across the city. Visitors wanting to enjoy foreign newspapers should visit the news kiosk in the Globus Commercial Center, the shopping center under Independence Square on Kreschatik Street.

Internet

Internet coverage in Kiev is good. Hotels will have WiFi availability in rooms or a business lounge and is typically available free. Please check with your hotel when booking. Throughout the city WiFi connectivity is available with all restaurants, cafes and bars offering free WiFi to customers.

Kiev Borispol Airport offers free WiFi for travellers.

Language

Russian and Ukrainian are spoken universally. English is spoken in the hotels and some popular tourist destinations. Street signs, museum guides and publications are commonly in Russian and Ukrainian. Some restaurants will offer English menus.

Here are some useful Russian terms to master to make your stay more comfortable.

Hi *Privet*
Hello / Good afternoon *Dobryj denj*
Goodbye *Do svidania / Poka (informal)*
Yes / No *Da / Niet*
Do you speak English? *Vy govorite po anglijski?*
Please *Pazhalusta*
Thank you *Spasiba*
Entrance / Exit *Vhod / Vyhod*
t is Open / Closed *Otkryto / Zakryto*

Where? *Gde?*
How much does it cost? *Skoljko stoit?*
Where is the toilet? *Gdie tualet?*
I don't speak Russian *Ya nie govorju po russki*
Can I have the bill? *Shchiot pazhalusta*
Excuse me *Proshu proscheniya*
I`m sorry *Izvinitie*
Nice to meet you *Priyatno poznakomitsia*
I don`t understand *Ya ne ponimayu*
I need a doctor *Mnie nuzhen doctor*
Can I use your phone *Ja mogu pozvonitj s vashego telefona?*
I'm lost *Ya poterialsia*
Help! *Pomogitie*
How are you? *Kak dela?*
My name is... Menia zovut...

We recommend the Lonely Planet Russian Phrasebook & Dictionary (USD8.45 on Amazon http://amzn.to/2jnPwMM, GBP4.99 http://amzn.to/2ixVKFb).

For those keen to master the mother tongue, here are the same phrases in Ukrainian. Russian is the main language spoke in Kiev, however many locals will appreciate your attempts to speak Ukrainian. The further west you travel the more widely Ukrainian has been adopted as the first language.

Hi *Pryvit*
Hello / Good afternoon *Dobryj denj*
Goodbye *Poka (informal), Do pobachennia*
Yes / No *Tak / Ni*
Do you speak English? *Vy rozmovliaiete anglijskoyu?*

Please *Budjlaska*
Thank you *Diakuiu*
Entrance / Exit *Vyhod / Vyhid*
It is Open / Closed *Zakryto / Zachyneno*
Where? *De?*
How much does it cost? *Skilky koshtuye?*
Where is the toilet? *De tualet?*
I don't speak Russian/Ukrainian
Ya ne rozmovliayu rosijskoyu/ukrainskoyu
Can I have the bill? *Rahunok budjlaska*
Excuse me *Probachte*
I'm sorry *Vibachte*
Nice to meet you *Priyemno poznayomitisya*
I don`t understand *Ya ne rozymiyo*
I need a doctor *Meni potriben likar*
Can I use your phone *Dozvolte zatelefonyvaty*
I'm lost *Ya zagybivsya*
Help! *Dopomozhyt!*
How are you? *Yak spravy?*
My name is... *Mene zvyt...*

Medical Emergencies

In a medical emergency please call an ambulance on 103 from anywhere in Ukraine or the Medicom Hospital (24 hour) 00380 44 503 7777. English-Russian translators can be organized emergencies or planned medical procedures.

Money

Hryvna (UAH), is the official currency of Ukraine.
At the time of writing (January 2017) the exchange rate

from UAH and US Dollars was 28.5 UAH to the Dollar.

Bills are issued in denominations of 1, 2, 5, 10, 20, 50, 100, 200 and 500 hryvnas while coins, called kopiyka, are issued in denominations of 1, 2 ,5 10, 25, and 50 kopiykas. One kopiyka is equal to 1/100 hryvnia.

Hryvnia can be easily exchanged to most major currencies in any bank branch.

The city is dotted with yellow currency exchange kiosks which offer competitive rates for US Dollar, Euro, UK Pound and Russian rouble exchange.

Foreign exchange kiosks typically feature yellow electric indicator boards "ОБМІН ВАЛЮТ" showing the current currency exchange rate for USD/UAH, EUR/UAH, RUB/UAH.

Kiev has four 24 hour kiosks for currency exchange around the clock.

Kreschatik Street 1/2, Hotel Dnipro, currency exchange kiosk

Velyka Zhytomirska Street, 2A, Hotel Intercontinental
Bessarabska sq.2, in front of Pinchuk Art Center, kiosk inside the market
Lesi Ukrainki boulevard 12, kiosk inside the food shop "Smachnyj"

Visa and Mastercard cards are accepted at most retailers while American Express is very rarely accepted. Visitors intending to use credit or debit cards in Ukraine should notify their bank prior to departure of their intention to travel to the country.

Travellers' cheques are not widely supported.

We recommend visitors to Kiev carry cash for convenience. You may bring USD or EUR as they are the most common in Ukraine and you may exchange those two currencies in banks or "currency exchange kiosks" at the airport, in the city or in your hotel lobby. British Pounds are less easy to change and British citizens would be advised to bring Euro.

Nightlife

The Kiev nightlife is a big draw for many tourists and the capital after dark doesn't disappoint. Expect Thursday, Friday and Saturday nights to be busiest. Some clubs, like D.Fleur, are open only on those days, while others party all week, several are even open 24 hours, operating in mornings as lounge bars.

There is usually no entry charge for ladies (or up to USD5) while men can expect to pay USD10-15. Drinks and cocktails vary are between USD 5-7 each, while a beer will set you back USD2.5-3.

The most popular and famous clubs in Kiev are:

SkyBar Club

Address: 5 Velyka Vasylkivska St

Telephone: +38 044 223 8888

Web: http:// skybar.ua/

Skybar is a centrally located nightclub walking distance from Kreschatik Street. The club boasts one of the best panoramic views of Kiev, original design and electro-pop music makes the club a popular destination for both locals and foreigners.

Caribbean Club

Address: 4 Symona Petliury St

Telephone: +38 067 224 4111

Web: http://caribbean.com.ua/en

A great Kiev club where you'll find an atmosphere to rival the top western clubs with fiery Latin rhythms and striking shows every night at midnight. This perennial favourite has been popular for generations. The club immediately established for quality music and friendly atmosphere and has retained its popularity with foreigners. Enjoy the music, marvel at the skill of the salsa dancers and enjoy great cocktails at the Caribbean Club.

Coyote Ugly

Address: 9A Mechnikova St

Telephone: +38 044 280 0678

One of the most popular bars in Kiev Coyote Ugly boasts a comfortable lounge and four large halls pulsating to the electro music beat and a heaving dance floor. Waitresses and female clubbers dance on the wooden bar. Coyote has a great friendly atmosphere and delicious drinks whch encourages everyone to dance till morning. Popular with students.

Buddha Bar

Address: 14 Khreschatik St

Telephone: +38044 270 7676

Web: http://en.buddhabar.com.ua/

Kiev's Buddha Bar is a popular pre-party lounge bar and restaurant, one of the network (also in Paris, Tokyo, New York, Beirut, Dubai, Cairo, Prague) and exudes a charmingly positive energy with cosy restaurant and relaxed lounge zone, inviting visitors to enjoy convivial atmosphere and enjoy the Buddha bar experience.

Serebro

Address: 3 Mechnikova St

Telephone: +380 96 303 0000

Serebro offers a 'two-in-one' club and karaoke experience under one roof. Conveniently located near the Arena Entertainment Complex at the end of Kreschatik Street, Serebro is the ideal getaway for those tired of the the electro beats and loud music offered by the other clubs. Enjoy the karaoke or a quiet drink before returning to the dancefloor!

D.Fleur Club

Address: 3 Mykhaila Hrushevskogo St

Telephone: +38 044 200 9009

D.Fleur, formerly know as DLux, is a contemporary party-restaurant. Under its former name it garnered a good reputation for a great sound system popular with pop and electro fans.

Personal Safety

While Kiev is generally a safe city for international visitors we would recommend tourists exercise the normal caution and awareness when visiting busy locations and after dark.

We recommend carrying no more than 2000 UAH (USD 72) in cash per day. ATM machines are plentiful and many retailers and restaurants accept cards.

Beware of pickpockets and petty thieves in busy public areas, especially those popular with tourists.

If you do encounter any difficulties call the police on the free call number 102 or (+38 044) 256 10 02/04.

Please always consult Ukraine travel advisories issued by your government for timely guidance on travel especially for onward journeys to the east of the country.

Police

The Ukrainian police service was reformed in 2015 following years of corruption claims. The 'new' police as they are locally known were US-trained in a hope to hold warranted officers to a higher standard. If you require police assistance anywhere in Ukraine, dial 102.

Public Holidays

Visitors to Kiev can expect some shops, most banks and all government agencies to be closed on public holidays. The present public holidays are observed:

New Year's Day 1 January
Orthodox Christmas 7 January
International Women's Day 8 March
Orthodox Easter - April (dates vary)
Labour Day 12 May
Victory Day (1945) 9 May
Constitution Day 28 June
Independence Day (1991) 24 August

Public Transport

Kiev has an excellent transport infrastructure, with buses, small private buses called marshrutka, trams, trolley buses and metro (subway) with 4 lines. The Kiev metro is easy to navigate and has signs in English. The cost of a single trip on the metro is 4 UAH / USD 0.14 (14c!) . See the metro map at http://go2ua.com/menus/view/maps.

Longer trips to the city suburbs frequently require more than one mode of public transport which can prove daunting to the visitors.

Metro tickets can only be purchased from the cashier at a Metro station. Up to four one way tickets can be purchased at a time, or a weekly ticket. Metro 'tickets' are issued in the form of plastic coins called 'zheton'. When you enter the metro station and deposit you zheton coin you are free to travel any distance. The weekly tickets are issued as weekly passes and need to be scanned to validate when entering the station. They do not need to be scanned on exit.

The Kiev metro has three lines and three interchange stations. The three colour coded lines are:

Line 1 Sviatoshynsko-Brovarska (Red Line)
running east-west
Line 2 Kurenivsko-Chervonoarmiyska (Blue Line)
running north-south
Line 3 Syretsko-Pecherska (Green Line)
running north west-south east

The interchange station of Maidan Nezalezhnosti – Kreschatik (for transfer between the blue and red lines) is the adjacent to the Independence Square, the main square at the beginning of the Kreschatik, the city's main street.

The other interchange stations are:
Zoloti Vorota – Teatralna (Green / Red Line)
Palats Sportu - Ploshcha Lva Tolstoho (Green / Blue Line)

The main train station in Kiev, for intercity rail travel, is located adjacent to the Vokzalna metro station, three stops to the west of the Maidan Nezalezhnosti station on the red line.

The Kiev Metro map can be found at later in this book.

There are no metro or rail connection to Kiev airports.

We would recommend for comfort and convenience tourists consider using the inexpensive Kiev taxi service.

Restaurants

The average restaurant bill in a Kiev restaurant, including wine, will be USD15-35. Kiev restaurants do take bookings however reservation are not normally required and staff seldom speak English.

We would encourage visitors to ask hotel concierge staff or their tour guide to make reservations when necessary. Some restaurants popular with tourists will offer an English-language menu.

It is customary, but not mandatory, to provide a 10% tip for good restaurant service.

Hutorets na Dnipri (Ukrainian Cuisine)
Address: 10A Naberezhno-Khreshchatytska street
Phone: +38 067 209 1444
Average Price: 600 UAH ($21)
Hutorets na Dnipri is traditional Ukrainian family restaurant housed in ship in the popular waterfront district of Podol. Diners can expect a river view and authentic Ukrainian dishes served in a distinct style.

Pervak (Ukrainian Cuisine)
Address: Rognedinskaya street, 2
Telephone: +38 044 235 0952
Average Price: 400 UAH ($15)
English Menu Available
Pervak is one of the best and oldest folk Ukrainian restaurants in Kiev located in the heart of the capital. Pervak, a favourite among locals and visitors, offers a wide range of traditional Ukrainian food and drinks which you can enjoy in a communal dining hall or one of the many small rooms decorated in Ukrainian style.

Ostannya Barykada (Ukrainian Cuisine)
Address: Globus Shopping Mall, 1 Maidan Nezalezhnocti

Telephone: +380 68 907 1991
Average Price: 400 UAH ($15)
English Menu Available
Ostannya Barykada or 'Last Barricade' is a new Kiev restaurant in the heart of the Kiev within the Globus Mall beneath the central city Maidan Square. The restaurant has a number of mementos to mark the revolutionary history of Kiev, from the ruins of the 11th century Liadskiy gate to the modern day revolutions. The restaurant has a relaxed lounge feel, cosy atmosphere and comfortable seating and serves popular Ukrainian dishes.
The restaurant has quickly established itself as a popular destination for Kievans so book ahead to avoid disappointment. A great selection of quality of dishes, excellent service, english speaking staff, a convenient central location and live evening folk music performances all make this an inviting destination for diners in the city.

Shynok (Ukrainian Cuisine)
Address: 28v Lesi Ukrainki Boulevard
Telephone: +38 044 2855777
Average Price: 300 UAH ($10)
The unique venue housed in a round tower doubles as a museum and seeks to recreate Ukrainian village life from the 19th century. The restaurant offers quality service, classical Ukrainian cuisine and attentive wait staff in national Ukrainian costume.

Vino e Cucina Restaurant (Italian Cuisine)
Address: 82 Sichovykh Stril'tsiv St
Telephone +38 067 823 82 82
Average Price: 800 UAH ($28)
English Menu Available

Restaurant Vino e Cucina is a large Italian restaurant with its own enoteca with an enviable collection of over 1000 bottles of wine and one of the best Italian menus in Kiev. This well appointed restaurant serves traditional Italian cuisine, and boasts excellent service and an cosy relaxing atmosphere. Restaurant Vino e Cucina is located 10 minutes drive from the heart of the capital, in a detached two-storey building and outdoor garden. The restaurant also has a dedicated 'kids zones'. A favourite with westerners, business people or those looking for a comfortable warm and welcoming environment to escape the elements.

BAO (Chinese)
Address: 14 Mechnikova St
Telephone +38 044 221 06 26
Average Price: 700-800 UAH ($25-28)
BAO was the first Kiev restaurant to offer modern Chinese cuisine. Each evening BAO echoes to the beat of popular music from the best Ukrainian DJs as guests enjoy original cocktails crafted by BAO's expert mixologists.The restaurant is owned by a famous TV show artist-chef who surprises with new ways of cooking and serving and is famous for a unique meals and quirky style.

Under Wonder (French, Italian Cuisine)
Address: 21 Velyka Vasylkivska St
Telephone: +38 044 234 21 81
Average Price: 500 UAH ($18)
Under Wonder is located close to Bessarabka Square, Arena city and Gulliver Shopping Mall at the end of Kreschatik Street. Under Wonder is a newcomer to the Kiev restaurant scene but has already become a favourite among Kievans. Located in the heart of the city Under Wonder is excellent

*venue for breakfast, a business lunch, or meetings friends. You
find great meat dishes and drinks with tasty desserts.*

Beef Meat & Wine (American, European)

Address: 11 Shota Rustaveli St
Telephone: +38 044 225 0035
Average Price: 800 UAH ($24)

*Beef Meat & Wine is a premium restaurant in central Kiev.
This is one of the best steak restaurants in the city with meat
specially imported to ensure the best culinary experience.
Befitting its name the menu is dominated by many cuts of meat
complemented by extensive wine list. Diners can select from
beef, pork, lamb, ostrich, duck dishes.
The main feature of this contemporary restaurant is the open
kitchen which enables guests to witness chefs preparing dishes
live.*

Alaska Restaurant (Mediterranean)

Alaska is a modern upmarket restaurant that opened
in 2017. The restaurant has a friendly and inviting
atmosphere. Whether you're enjoying a juicy steak or
king crab's feet, Alaska is a great destination for hungry
travellers and is a welcome escape from the bustling city
streets that surround the location.
*Address: 20 Sichovykh Stril'tsiv St
Telephone: +380 99 521 3777
Average Price: 700 UAH ($25)*

Katuska Restaurant (Soviet)

Katuska is a chain of restaurants serving old fashioned
Soviet-style cuisine. Famous for its dumplings, crepes,
traditional salads and soups, fruit desserts. cottage cheese,
baked cakes and soviet era staples. Prices are relatively

cheap at this restaurant with the Soviet style interior makes diners feel like they're dining in the USSR.

Address: 29/1 Kreschatik St
Telephone: +380 44 235 9335
Average Price: 250 UAH ($9)

Restaurant recommendations are based on the author's dining experience, feedback from clients of Go2UA tours, Trip Advisor and Google Reviews.

This information was not sponsored and is intended as a guide only. Restaurants were selected based on experience and location, reputation, appearance and food.

Taxis

Taxis are a popular way to navigate the city and are inexpensive compared to many European or US cities. A type one-way fare from the city to a suburb would be USD 4, however expect to pay upwards of USD 30 for an airport transports.

Kiev welcomed Uber in 2016 and this service is growing in popularity.

For convenience and English language support we would recommend visitors to Kiev use Uber or the local UKLon service (uklon.com.ua). Sign up to Uber in Kiev with this link: http://www.uber.com/t2gui.

Telephones

The Ukraine country code is +380.

Mobile telephone coverage in the city is good, however data roaming charges outside of the European Union are high.

If you need to use a mobile phone during your stay we would suggest you consider buying a prepaid Ukrainian SIM card from a local telecommunications company such as KyivStar (https://kyivstar.ua) or Vodafone Ukraine (https://www.vodafone.ua/en). Both companies have retail stores throughout the city.

Visitors to Ukraine from USA and Canada should be aware that, like the rest of continental Europe, Ukraine mobile providers operates on a GSM network, so it is likely that many North American cell phones will not work in Ukraine.

We recommend consulting your cell provider prior to travel or purchasing an inexpensive cellphone and SIM card.

There was no 4G in Ukraine at the time of writing (January 2018) although carriers have indicated 4G services will be introduced in late 2018.

Time

Kiev is +1 hours ahead of western continental Europe and +2 hours ahead of United Kingdom and Portugal. From the last Sunday in March to the final Sunday in October, Ukraine enjoys summer time, where clocks move forward.

What to wear

Kiev's many shopping centres and markets sell affordable winter clothes for those looking for a shopping adventure!

We recommend two shopping centres for clothes shopping: Globus Trade Complex, underground at Independence Square on Kreschatik Street in the city centre (http://www.globus.com.ua/), and Gulliver Shopping Centre, Sportyvna pl. 1A, Kiev 01601 (http://gullivercenter.com/) open 10am-10pm daily.

Where to Stay

Kiev has an abundance of hotels to suit all tastes, from five star opulence to budget options for the price conscious traveller. The capital's hotels are cheaper than many of their western European counterparts so visitors should find their budget stretches further in Kiev. The Hyatt, Hilton and Intercontinental hotels offer five star luxury in the heart of the city, while more affordable four star comfort is offered at the Radisson Blue Kiev and Kreschatik Hotel located in the heart of the city.

For more advise on where to stay in Kiev and an up-to-date list of the best hotels for foreign visitors see http://go2ua.com/hotels.

Most hotels will offer a light breakfast, consisting of fruit, tea, coffee, cold meats, pancakes. Breakfast is not normally including in the standard price per night and is ordered and paid additionally. The average hotel breakfast cost is USD20 while restaurants offer comparable breakfasts for USD3-5.

We would recommend visitors consult independent hotel reviews on TripAdvisor when evaluating all hotels in Ukraine.

An affordable alternative to booking a hotel in Kiev, especially for longer stays, is to rent an apartment in the city. As with hotels, apartments are plentiful and quality varies, so be sure to read reviews closely. When inspecting apartments it is wise to perform routine checks of hot water, water pressure, lighting and routine maintenance before paying for your accommodation. It is customary to pay a holding deposit for the apartment website and the remainder in cash to the apartment owner upon arrival. Some of the popular websites for booking apartments in Kiev are dobovo.com, podobovo.com.ua, doba.ua/kiev, airbnb.com and booking.com.

Tipping

Tipping is common in Ukraine and has begun to be observed in restaurants where a 10% tip is customary for good service.

Toilets

Public toilets are in short supply but are free. All shopping centres will have free toilet facilities. Male toilets are marked by an upside down triangle, Ч or M (meaning cholovichy or muzhcheny), while female toilets are depicted by an upwards-facing triangle or Ж (for zhinochy).

Some toilets will have attendants and all paid toilet facilities will accept cash, in the local currency, only.

MAPS

To help orientate newcomers to Kiev we have provided a collection of helpful maps of the central city district.

Ukrainian lawmakers routinely rename popular streets from Russian to Ukrainian or to reflect modern Ukraine and expunge Soviet history and traditional street names. This makes navigating the city a challenge at times so we recommend tech-savvy travellers to use Google Maps as a reliable and up-to-date directions.

As a bonus for readers we have exclusive electronic access to Kiev's most popular illustrated tourist map which is available at over 40 central city hotels, Borispol and Zhuliany airport tourist information desks and best restaurants in the city.

To view the illustrated 3D map, courtesy of Grata Apartments, visit http://accommodation.kiev.ua/images/artmap.jpg and a print-ready A4 Kiev street map http://accommodation.kiev.ua/pages/kyiv-map-eng.pdf.

The metro network map shows the three lines and 52 stations on the Kiev network. The metro runs from 0600 to 2400 daily. For more information on using the metro see the public transport section.

KIEV
METRO MAP

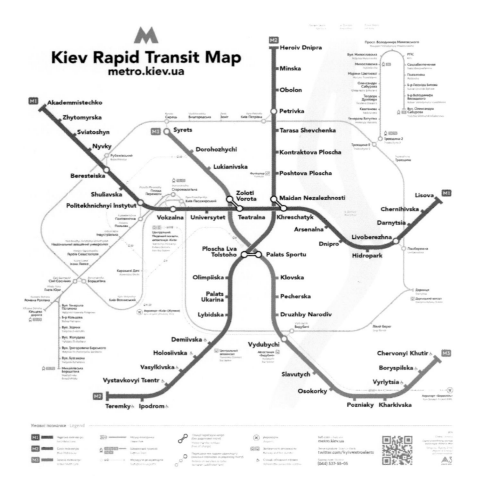

KIEV
SIGHTS OF INTEREST

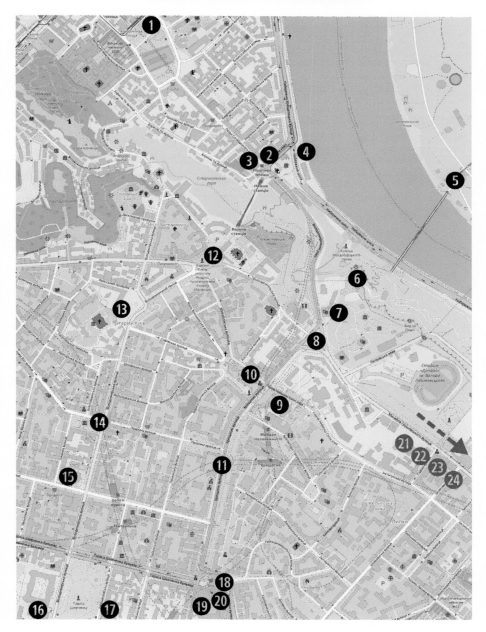

1. Kontractova Square

Old city centre in Podil. Popular night spot with restaurants and bars.

2. Poshtova Square

Riverside square from where you can take a boat trip or walk across a footbridge to Trukhaniv Island.

3. Funicular

Cable car to upper town and St Michael's cathedral.

4. Boat trips

Boat trips depart from here in the summer months and depending on weather conditions.

5. Trukhaniv Island

Beach clubs, Bike hire, outdoor activities.

6. Arch of Friendship

Great view across towards Podil, river and Left Bank. A Soviet monument to a united nation.

7. National Philharmonic

Music concert halls.

8. European Square

Gateway to the central city district.

9. Globus Mall

An underground shopping centre with food courts, restaurant and supermarket beneath Maidan Square and adjacent to metro station.

10. Majdan / Independence Square

The central square and traditional meeting place for Kiev.

11. Kreschatik Street

The main street of the capital.

12. St. Michael Church

Golden Domed Monastery.

13. St. Sophia Cathedral

11th century Unesco heritage site famous for frescoes and mosaics.

14. Golden Gate

Principal ceremonial entrance to the old city in the 11th century.

15. Opera House

National Opera & Ballet performances daily during "open" season.

16. T. Shevchenko University

17. Russian Arts Gallery

Largest collection of Russian arts and paintings in Ukraine.

18. Bessarabska Square

Food market.

19. Arena City

Clubs, Restaurants, Cafes, Boutiques, Supermarket, Parking.

20. Pinchuk Art Centre

Modern Arts gallery. Temporary exhibitions. Free entry.

21. Cave monastery Lavra

(UNESCO) 11th century heritage site famous for its over 800m of tunnels dug through centuries by monks.

22. World War II museum

World War II museum with wide array of armory and equipment. 3 floors.

23. Motherland Statue

Soviet monument soaring high over the city. A viewing platform from atop the shield offers panoramic views across the city.

24. Miniatures museum

An engineering marvel. Art seen only through a magnifying glass.

OTHER BOOKS IN THE SERIES

Essential Lviv Guide (2018 Edition) will be published in spring 2018 as a companion guide to this publication. For readers wishing to receive an advanced copy of the Lviv Guide please email welcome@go2ua.com to be put on the publication mailing list to be the first to know.

ACKNOWLEDGEMENTS

Ilya Bogin (flic.kr/p/2meniY)
Jean & Nathalie (flic.kr/p/5iqF5h)
Bossi (flic.kr/p/6XnHNN)
Giles Thomas (flic.kr/p/8AAv3t)
Loris Silvio Zecchinato (flic.kr/p/8DZzoQ)
Ilya (flic.kr/p/8U9gFS)
Jennifer Boyer (flic.kr/p/a6B41P, flic.kr/p/a7SB6P,
flic.kr/p/a7SoSH)
Sergey Galyonkin (flic.kr/p/apoN41)
Christopher Irvin (flic.kr/p/bf6ykT)
Irisina (flic.kr/p/d5DE2w)
Jorge Láscar (flic.kr/p/e77Nid)
Michele Ursino (flic.kr/p/eerf5K)
Marko Knuutila (flic.kr/p/g9VTrE)
Adam Jones (flic.kr/p/GNpidW)
Deep Stereo (flic.kr/p/kwfQx4)
Alexxx Malev (flic.kr/p/mjdMSH)
Juanedc (flic.kr/p/wPw8p9)

Photographs reproduced under the
Creative Commons commercial license.

Printed in Great Britain
by Amazon